MW00508847

Junia

Gentle Soul of the Holocaust

Biography

Written and Illustrated by

Holly Harlayne Roberts, D.O., PhD

Anjeli Press, Inc.

Junia

Gentle Soul of the Holocaust

Biography
Written and Illustrated by

Holly Harlayne Roberts, D.O., PhD

Published by Anjeli Press, Inc.
www.AnjeliPress.com

ISBN 978-09799244-7-7

Printed in the United States
by Lightning Source
Distributed by Ingram Distributors

Dedicated to

Junia Baum Katz

Zlata Baum

Ira Katz

and millions
of other innocent victims
of the Holocaust.

Introduction

Junia Baum was just twelve years of age when German soldiers began their march into Poland. Hers had been a life full of love, kindness, and family bonding. She knew little of hate, prejudice, racism, and anti-Semitism, and even less about the potential harm that lay within man's inhumanity to man.

Her world had revolved around the family members, her parents, sister, aunts, uncles, cousins, and grandparents, living in the cluster of three houses her grandfather had built. It revolved also around the small one-room synagogue that her grandfather had created at the rear of this cluster.

The people who inhabited Junia's town were one-third Polish, one-third Ukrainian, and one-third Jewish. Although anti-Jewish pogroms during the late nineteenth century had led to the murder of thousands of Jews throughout Poland and Russia, the citizens of her town generally coexisted quite well. For the most part, residents of the town knew their place, and each respected the space of others.

Young Junia could not have possibly imagined that in neighboring Germany, plans were being made to annihilate each and every one of the nine million defenseless Jewish men, women, and children throughout the entire continent of Europe. To eliminate, somehow, absolutely every Jew everywhere!

How could such a plan have evolved and taken root? The roots of anti-Semitic prejudice date back over two thousand years. During the first century C. E., the Romans had seized control of the Holy Lands. During that century, through slaughter and starvation, they murdered 600,000 Jews. For centuries to follow, Jews were blamed for the death of one of their own, Joshua, known to us today as Jesus, the Christ. Even the thousands of Jews who lived outside the Holy Lands during that century were blamed for his death.

During the early twentieth century, Germany was suffering financial difficulties due to heavy war reparations. It was forced to pay these for its part in World War I. The time was ripe for Hitler, chancellor of Germany, a man with many emotional problems, to rally the German people to place the blame for their problems on the Jews.

Hitler preached that Jews were a subhuman species (*Untermenschen*) that had invaded the human race, and needed to be eliminated. This was ironic because Jews had been filling a disproportionately large number of positions as professors, physicians and attorneys throughout Germany, even though they represented less than one percent of Germany's population. In addition, they won almost a third of the Nobel Prizes that had been awarded to Germans.

It was even more ironic because the individuals that citizens of Germany and the other Christian European nations revered, Jesus, Mary, and Joseph, were Jews.

Hitler defined his beliefs in 1924, in *Mein Kampf* (*My Struggle*), a book he wrote in prison. It is a virulent anti-Semitic work in which he declares the Nordic-Aryan-German race the "master race" and Jews the worst enemy of this master race. He declared that in the interest of national racial purity, Jews must be eliminated.

Yet it was not Hitler alone, nor Germany alone, that made possible the senseless slaughter of six million of Europe's nine million Jews. It was the cumulative effect of centuries of religious, social, economic, and racial anti-Semitism that did. It was this institutionalized anti-Semitism, in Germany, Poland, the European states within the former Soviet Union, Czechoslovakia, Hungary, Lithuania, Holland, France, Greece, Yugoslavia, Latvia, Austria, Rumania, Belgium, Italy, Estonia, Norway, Luxembourg, Albania, and Crete, that permitted the depraved mass slaughter of thousands of Jewish men, women, children, and infants to occur in each of these countries.

In spite of all of these atrocities, eventually, one must make peace within oneself concerning the Holocaust, or one cannot go on. One need not forget, but one must make peace. Junia is one who has done so. Although she suffered the full impact of the holocaust, she wishes ill towards no one. Her heart is full of love for all people and all nations, and she feels peace in knowing that the richness of her beloved faith, the Jewish faith, could not be destroyed, and will live on.

This is her story.

Junia

Gentle Soul of the Holocaust

Junia's story actually began long ago.
Very long ago.

It began over five thousand years ago
with her ancient ancestors.
They were members of a fine family,
a family that lived in the ancient Middle East.

They went by the names of
Abram, Sarai, Terah, and Lot.

They were Semitic people.
They had:
beautiful olive skin,
the pigment of which protected their skin from
the harmful penetrating rays of the sun.

They had dark, wavy hair
that blocked the heat of the sun
from burning their scalps.

And they had strong high-bridged noses,
the passages of which added humidity
to the dry desert air they breathed,
and protected their lungs
from becoming parched.

Five thousand years ago,
these ancestors
left the land of their birth,
known as the lands between the two rivers,
the Tigris and the Euphrates,
and traveled westward.

They left the city of their birth, Ur,
because God had spoken to Abram
and told him:

"Go forth from your native land
and from your father's house
to the land that I will show you.
I will make of you a great nation,
and I will bless you."
Torah, Genesis 12:1-2

So Abram went forth with his family
as God had commanded.

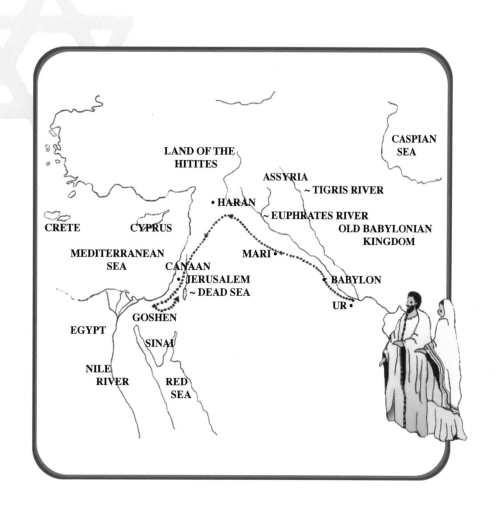

Over the centuries,
God created many challenges
for Abram and his descendants,
and they were forced to leave the lands
God promised them
and wander to distant lands.

Their wanderings began in 722 BCE,
when Assyrians invaded their lands.
Again, in 586 BCE,
their people were carried to distant lands
by invading Babylonians.
And once again, in 70 CE,
invading Romans conquered their lands,
and forced most surviving individuals
to leave their homes,
not to return for almost 2,000 years.

Over the millenia,
Junia's ancestors,
having been forced to leave their homeland,
traveled to many distand lands—
lands to the east, the west,
the north, and the south.

Some migrated directly north,
along the western border of the Black Sea.
And that was how Junia's people
ended up in the region they did,
in the small Polish town
called Boryslaw.

From 1860 to 1914,
these lands were ruled
by the Austro-Hungarian Empire.
Later, they were annexed by Poland.

To the Jews living there, however,
these lands were known as "Galicia."

Before World War II,
half a million Jews lived there.

At the present time,
these lands are part of the Ukraine.

Today, the term Galicia is no longer used.
It is just a memory in history books.

Very few Jews live there today.

Boryslaw was a small town in Galicia.
It was at the foothills
of the Carpathian Mountains.

In 1939, during the early phases of the Holocaust,
one third of the town's inhabitants were Polish,
one third were Ukrainian,
and one third were Jewish.

At that time,
15,000 Jews lived in Boryslaw.

Similar to other towns
in this region,
Boryslaw was a mere cluster of small houses
joined by unpaved roads.
Each spring, the snow melted
from the impressive mountain peaks,
and the lands flooded.

A railway line joined Boryslaw
to the larger cities to the east.
But the rail line was forced to end in Boryslaw,
blocked by
the Carpathian Mountains.

In Boryslaw,
the soil was dark brown, clumpy, and sticky.
Crops and well water had an unpalatable flavor.
The reason for this was that the soil
was filled with crude oil.

In 1853, a young Jew named Abraham Schreiner
analyzed that the soil of Boryslaw
was filled with oil.
He noted that as the soil became dry,
it yielded a wax-like substance.
This substance could be made to burn.
As it burned, it filled the rooms with soot.

With the help of a Polish engineer,
he drilled the first oil well.
This was the founding of the oil industry.

Because of this thriving oil industry,
a distinct odor permeated the entire town,
and many miles of fields surrounding it.

Many people, not native to Boryslaw,
might not have liked it there.
But to Junia and her family
it was home.

By 1920,
Boryslaw supplied 75% of the oil
consumed in Poland.

With success, however,
came competition.

Foreign businessmen funded by large banks
came to town.
They squeezed out the small, local owners
of the oil companies.
The local people were forced to work
from dawn to dusk to eke out a living.

The working masses
suffered poverty and deprivation.
The government supported large businesses,
thus making it impossible
for small businesses to sustain.
This affected the Jewish population in particular.

Anti-Semitic policies by the government
did not permit Jews employment
in the large institutions or factories.
They also did not permit Jews
to receive unemployment insurance.

Junia's parents were hard working people.
Junia's mother, Zlata Lerner, was born in 1901.
At the age of twenty-five,
she married Beno Baum.
He was seven years her elder.
The marriage had been arranged by her father.

Beno was a serious, quiet, clean-cut man.
He was refined and well-educated.
He worked in a family business
that transported lumber for use in the oil industry.

Their lives had been peaceful.
Yet as people of Jewish heritage,
they remained cautious.
Zlata and Beno were blessed with two children,
Lucia and Junia.

Every day, Junia walked to school in the town.
But she recognized that those students
who were not Jewish
received higher grades than those who were,
for lower levels of performance.
She just accepted,
and dedicated herself to her studies at home.

Junia's life was fulfilled.
At home she had a serious, kind father,
a wise, sincere mother,
and a loving sister, Lucia, four years her senior.

Hers was a tight-knit family.
Her immediate family lived adjacent
to their extended family
in a complex of three houses.

The houses were surrounded on all sides
by a wooden fence.
A gated entrance, just large enough to permit
their carriage with its two horses
to pass through,
was located on one side of the fence.

Junia spent most of her days
within this small cluster of three houses,
amidst the love and acceptance
of her parents, older sister,
grandparents,
her aunts, Eva and Tonsha,
her uncles,
and her cousins.

Junia's maternal grandparents,
grandpa Isaac & grandma Sheve Lerner,
lived in a portion of her house.

At the rear of Junia's house was a special room.
It was a synagogue.
Junia's grandfather had created a
separate entrance for it.
He had fitted it with benches
and three Torahs -
two for the adults and one for the children.
He also had it blessed by a rabbi.

Thusly, he converted it into a tiny synagogue.

This family synagogue
was a holy sanctuary.
It became a sanctuary of love, peace,
and God.
For Junia's family,
it was a peaceful, holy, sacred spot.
Though their synagogue was small,
it was filled with love.

Junia's grandfather prayed in the synagogue
every day.

Junia had just reached twelve years of age
when everything began to change.

Jewish people from Austria and Germany,
even those people whose ancestors
had been living in these lands for centuries,
had been forced to flee.
They left their homes, farms, businesses,
towns, and cities
and, in desperation,
fled to the east.

Droves of them flocked into Junia's town.
They told of terrible atrocities
having been inflicted
upon the Jewish citizens in their towns.
They told of synagogues being burned,
shops and homes looted and torched,
Jewish cemeteries desecrated,
and Jewish schools destroyed.
They told of Jews being attacked on the streets,
dragged from their homes,
robbed, beaten, shot, and murdered.

All the news was distressing beyond belief.

On September 1, 1939,
Germany invaded Poland.
It was then that bombs first fell on Boryslaw,
the town in which Junia lived.

German soldiers overran the town.
Within a mere few days, Poland fell.
Initially, Russia had been an ally of Germany.
Russia and Germany made a pact
to divide Poland between them.
Eastern Poland, including Boryslaw,
was given to the Russians.

So after the Germans
had been in Boryslaw three days,
the Russians marched in.

In the short time the Germans were there,
they terrorized the Jewish people.
They beat, kicked and clubbed them,
ransacked Jewish homes,
liquidated Jewish businesses,
robbed hundreds of small Jewish merchants
of their means of sustenance,
and made survival for Jews almost hopeless.

Rationing was instituted in such a way that it was
almost impossible for Jews to get food.
Jewish organizations were outlawed.
The Jewish press was muzzled.

When the Russians marched in,
they led groups of Jewish people to Siberia.
They took Junia's girlfriend and her family
to Siberia.

At first,
the friendship between Russia and Germany
was strong.
Stalin sought to win favor with Hitler
so as to obtain part of Poland.
He paid Hitler with millions of dollars
in the form of food, oil, and other goods.
Germany needed these to conduct war.

The Russians told Junia's parents
that because their family was financially well off,
they were on "a list" to go to Siberia.
They might be abducted at any time.
Junia had to stop going to school,
and even stop going outside.
She had just reached 6th grade.

June 22, 1941, Hitler attacked Russia.
The Russians were forced to leave Poland.
But as they left Boryslaw,
they set the oil wells on fire.
Flames rose up and plumes of smoke filled the sky.
It seemed as though the heavens turned black.
An omen of things to come.
When the Russians left,
they transported more of the Jews to Siberia.

Between June 30 and July 3, 1941,
the Germans took Boryslaw.
They gave free reign to the Ukrainians,
who joined them in attacking, torturing,
and murdering Jewish citizens.
For three days, mobs attacked the Jews.
The Germans told the elders
of the Jewish community, the Judenrat,
to tell the Jews that
if they brought their silver and other valuables,
to be given to the Germans,
their lives would be spared.

So Junia's father, Beno, loaded all the silver the
family owned into a sack
to bring to the Judenrat.

At the same time, however,
the Ukrainians were viciously attacking all Jews
with pitchforks, axes,
and whatever else they could use as a weapon.
After three days,
many Jewish men, women and children
had been killed, and hundreds badly injured.
It rained heavily,
as if Heaven wept for the Jewish blood
that was flowing.

On the road to the Judenrat,
Beno was attacked, robbed, kicked,
and severely beaten by the Ukranians.
After they beat him, they left him to die.
They tossed his limp body in a pile of bodies of
other dying and dead Jews.

Still alive,
yet gasping for air and bleeding heavily,
Beno noticed a young boy walking among the bodies.
He wrote a few words
on the paper from a cigarette butt.
He wrote these with his own blood.
Then he gave the tiny paper to the young boy
to carry back to his family.

When Zlata and Junia read the tiny note,
they ran with it to the Judenrat.
They found Beno and carried him home.
He was coughing and choking,
and could not walk.
His ribs had been broken,
he was covered with blood,
and he had great difficulty breathing.

The next day, the Germans marched into town
in massive numbers.
They marched with straight legs,
stern faces, and piercing eyes.

They instituted a "pogrom."
In this pogrom, they pulled rabbis into the streets,
kicked, beat, shot and killed them.
They set the synagogues on fire,
trashed Jewish homes, and looted Jewish shops.

All Jews were ordered to come into the streets.
Some tried to hide,
but their Ukrainian and Polish neighbors
pointed to where they were hiding,
and shouted to the Germans,
"Here are the Jews! Here are the Jews!"

Zlata knew they needed to hide.
The Germans would spare no Jew.

She thought: The attic!
They could hide in the tiny attic!
She tried to bring Beno
into the attic,
but he was too weak.
He had been too badly beaten by the Ukrainians.

She and Junia hugged him,
and rushed to climb the tiny ladder above the hall
and hide in their narrow attic.
There was just enough room to lie down.

Both Zlata and Junia hid
lying on their abdomens in this tiny space.
They stayed in total silence,
barely breathing.

All was silent.
Too silent.
Then they heard noise.
The loud, rough voices of German soldiers.
The stomping of boots.
The harsh thrashing around of objects.

The Germans found Junia's father, Beno.
They dragged him out and threw him in a truck.
They took him to L'viv, shot him,
and threw his body in a ditch.
This was the same ditch in which his father's body
had been thrown after WW I.

Then, Junia and Zlata
heard screams, pleas, and sobs.
The Germans had caught Junia's cousin, Fania,
and her two small children,
her seven-year-old son Kubish,
and four year old daughter Soisha,
hiding in the stable.

Fania cried, "Come, come my Kubish, my Soisha!
We must go for our last walk!"

They dragged Fania and her two small children,
beat Fania, shoved her and her children into a truck,
and took them to a camp.
There, they killed them.

In their attic hiding place,
Zlata and Junia remained frozen with fear.
Numb with panic.

The Jews of Boryslaw had been caught unaware.
How could they, in 1939, have ever anticipated
the Germans' hideous anti-Jewish policies?

Over two hundred and fifty Jews of Boryslaw
were killed in that pogrom.
Some were shot and thrown into the pit.
Others died later from their wounds.

All that day, and the following night,
the Germans, the Ukrainians, and then the Poles,
looted everything from the homes of the Jews.

Peasants from neighboring villages
joined those from Boryslaw
in terrorizing and killing Jews.
Using axes, hammers, and lead pipes,
they turned into a bloodthirsty mob.
Like animals,
they turned against Jewish neighbors
who had befriended them for years.
No human feeling.
No pity.
The more helpless the neighbor,
the greater their cruelty.

The day passed, and then the night.
Zlata and Junia remained hidden in the attic.
They heard a great deal of noise downstairs.
Sounds of boisterous clamor.
Rushes of footsteps.
Banging of furniture.
Then there was silence.

The following day,
they opened the hatch to their hiding place,
and came down.
Everything in their house was gone.
Everything!
Furniture, shutters, carpets, even the oven.
Everything was gone.

All that was left in Junia's home was blood.
Blood everywhere.
The trail of Junia's father's blood.

Zlata and Junia peered out of their windows.
They saw Germans
still pulling Jews from their homes,
chasing them as they tried to escape,
and beating them in the streets.

The Germans tormented the Jews
in the most demeaning fashion.
They brought them to the slaughter yard
to beat them and shoot them to death.
Men, women and children alike.
Then, they threw their bodies in the ditch.

The ditch was filled with corpses.
People had been so brutally beaten,
that their disfigured faces were unrecognizable.

Junia and Zlata could only sob.
What would happen next?
What was this all about?
Why?

During the following days, all was quiet.
Junia's sixteen-year-old sister, Lucia,
recently married,
rushed to see them.
She and her young husband survived.

Over the next two to three weeks,
all seemed quiet.
Yet a foreboding sense of doom
permeated the air.

All Jewish shops had been confiscated.
Food became scarce.
All Jews were to wear white armbands
embroidered with a blue Star of David.
To be caught without one,
meant death.

Other people looked at the Jews
with an air of superiority.
Some would not even look at them,
but merely turn away.
The beginning of a dehumanization process.

The Germans ordered the Judenrat
to supply Jews to work for them.
Some days Junia was ordered to knit sweaters.
Other days she was ordered to stay home.

Food was rationed.
Lines were impossibly long.
Zlata and Junia dug around their property
in hopes of finding potatoes.

Jews were not permitted to own radios.
No one knew exactly what was happening
or what would happen next.

November, 1941.
Germans began grabbing every Jew they could
off the streets.
Even those reporting to assigned work,
were carried off the streets.
The Germans beat them
with sticks, clubs, axes, and rifle butts.
The shrill screams of the beaten filled the air.
The second pogrom had begun.

Zlata and Junia rushed to hide in the basement of
Zlata's sister's house.
They lifted planks of wood up off the kitchen floor,
and slid down this opening into the cellar.
Then they replaced the planks from underneath.

It was cold, moist and dark.
They curled up—ever so quietly.
Then they heard steps above them.
Gruff, yelling voices.
"Where are the Jews! Where are the Jews!"
Shrieks, screams, sobs.
The Germans caught another one of Junia's aunts
and her two children.

They also caught and killed one hundred other Jews.

Among those the Germans caught
was Junia's sixteen-year old sister, Lucia.

She had wed just a short time prior,
and was living in another part of town.

The Germans caught her,
beat her severely,
shot her,
and threw her remains in the same pit
they had thrown Junia's father
six months earlier.

More pogroms followed.
And yet more.
Germans combed every inch of the town.

They sadistically tormented, beat, and killed
any Jewish man, woman, and child they caught.

Running, hiding, and dying.
More violence, more brutality, more questions.
The Jews could only ask, "Why?"

A cloud of unknowing permeated the air.
It pervaded everything.

The ghetto.
Winter of 1941 to 1942.
Word of an order spread.
The order was that all remaining Jews in Boryslaw
must leave their homes
and relocate to a ghetto.
A ghetto had been created
in the poorest part of town.
Zlata took Junia and walked there rapidly.
The houses in the ghetto were small
and many people were crammed into each.
Where were the original Jewish owners?
No one ever knew.

Guards stood at checkpoints.
A wall encircled the entire perimeter of the ghetto.
Farmers were not permitted to enter.
Food was extremely scarce.

As new groups of Jews
arrived at ghetto checkpoints,
some were immediately arrested.
It all seemed quite random.
No one knew where they were being taken.
Later, however, people knew.
They were taken to death camps.

Babies were snatched from their mother's arms.
Parents were jerked away from their children.
Small children were left to wander
around the ghetto alone.
Eventually, they, too, were taken.

Almost immediately
pogroms began in the ghetto!
Harsh German shouts.
All were to report to the central courtyard.
Go Right! Go Left! Go Right! Go Left!
(Life! Death! Life! Death!)
(Work! Annihilation! Work! Annihilation!)

Only those Jews the Germans could use as workers
were spared—
spared for the time being.

Zlata was an able bodied woman,
capable of hard labor.
But she feared for Junia's life.

Though twelve years of age,
Junia looked more like nine.
She was petite and thin,
and she bore the look of innocence upon her face.

Zlata knew that the Germans must not find Junia
during that, or during any future pogrom.
She would not be spared.
They would not consider her useful.

A fellow Jew
helped them crawl into a narrow space
under the floorboards.
Cold, moist, and teaming with insects, worms,
and rodents.
They inched themselves down.
They shimmied in contorted positions
and lay between the floor joists.

Not a movement. Not a word. Not a breath.
They must survive.

Sounds above.
Harsh German yelling.
Arrogant German footsteps.
Thrashing.
Opening. Closing. Slamming.
Trashing.

Screams, pleas, cries,
sobs.

March, 1942.

From inside their ghetto hiding spot,
they heard sounds.
These were the sounds
of automatic rifles and bullets.
The sounds came from all directions.
They were also the sounds
of truck engines revving up.

This was the first major transport of Jews
from Boryslaw
to the Belzec crematorium.
One thousand Jews.

The Germans filled their trucks
with innocent Jews.
Met their quota.

Mothers, fathers, grandparents,
teens, schoolchildren,
toddlers, infants, pregnant women.
The Germans' main goal - women, babies, children,
the old, the weak, the infirm.
Their trucks left the ghetto.
The first of many transports.

Zlata, Junia, and several others
remained under the floorboards.
Time passed. A day and a half.
The air was stifling. It was difficult to breathe.

Gradually, Zlata became delirious.
Lack of oxygen and extreme dehydration
had overtaken her.
She was semi-conscious.
Moving and mumbling.
She had become a danger to herself
and to the others.
She needed liquids.
Someone collected urine in a small cup,
held Zlata's nose so she could not smell it,
and had her drink it.
She survived.

Life went on in the ghetto.
For some.

But not for all.
Some starved to death,
some succumbed to pneumonia,
and some to typhus, dysentery, or tuberculosis.
Others were sent to the Belzec crematorium.

Treblinka
Chelmo
Sobibor
Maidanek
Auschwitz
Boryslaw
Belzec

Nations from which Jews were sent to concentration camps.

Nations from which no Jews were sent to their deaths.

Major concentration camps set up for the murder of Jews.

Major camps where Jews and non-Jews were starved, worked to death, tortured and murdered. Numerous smaller camps fed these.

Boryslaw: The town in which Zlata and Junia Baum lived.

August, 1942.
The pogroms continued.
Six thousand more Jews were taken.
All exterminated.

Zlata and Junia still clung to life.
Returning again and again
to their hiding spot under the floorboards.
For how long
could they surviive?

February 1943.
Six hundred Jews were packed into a movie house.
Packed to the point of suffocation.
Then, all were taken to the slaughterhouse.
All were shot.
All thrown into a pit.
All covered with soil.
Hours passed.
The earth kept heaving.
Those buried while still alive
struggled to disentangle themselves
from the mass of twisted arms and legs above them.
None could.

The earth seeped with blood.

It seemed hopeless.
Just hopeless.

Then, Zlata made a contact.
A cousin.
The cousin obtained papers
for both Junia and Zlata
to leave the ghetto.
Work papers to work at a labor camp
at an old military stable.

They were given an emblem with an "R"
to wear on their jackets.
"R" for "Reiterzug"
meaning "necessary worker."

They were permitted to leave the ghetto,
and to enter the work camp.

Just in time.
For the ghetto had suddenly been liquidated!
This meant that
each and every Jew in the ghetto was sent
to the crematorium at Belzec.
Even those who had been hiding with them
under the floorboards were caught, and killed.

A Polish man,
secretly among the "righteous gentiles"
seeking to save Jews
ran the work camp.
Although the Jews there had to work hard,
his efforts helped them survive.
When the German police, the Gestapo,
came to transport Jews to the crematorium,
he tried to save as many as he could.

Zlata was assigned to cook at the work camp
and Junia to clean rooms.
She was also taken each day to work
at a fiberglass factory.
She was fourteen years of age.
Fiberglass cut through the skin
of her arms and legs.
She was covered with open festering wounds.
Bloody pustules broke out all over her limbs.
Yet she was alive.

She wore the same clothes and same shoes
she wore the day of the first pogrom.
But here, she was given wads of cloth
to place inside her worn shoes.
This enabled her to survive the harsh winter.

At the work camp,
Junia and Zlata were given enough food
to sustain their strength and health.

They slept in beds with several other women,
and shared covers with them;
yet, life was bearable.

The days passed.
All was calm—relatively calm.

Then word leaked out that
the Germans were making plans
to liquidate the work camp.
The plan was to send all the Jews there
to Auschwitz.

They must leave quickly.
They must find a way out!

Zlata and Junia made a contact.
Three teenage boys, one young woman,
and an older couple.

The plan was made.
The older couple supplied the funds.

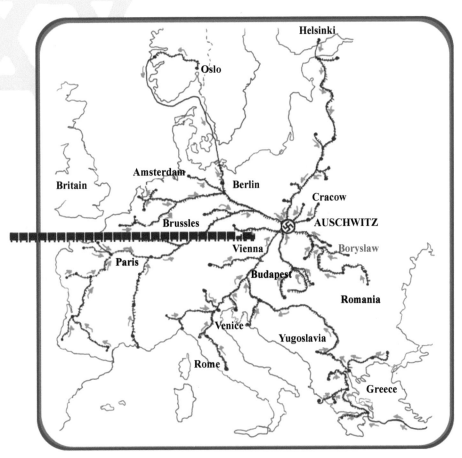

More than a million Jews were deported to Auschwitz and
murdered there. Most of them - including all women and children - were killed in the gas chambers within a few hours of
their arrival. Tens of thousands of others were forced to work
as slave laborers and then killed when they became too ill or
weak to work. Fewer than ten thousand survived.

Evening.
The sky was pitch black.

Silently,
each of the eight
crept through a tear in the fence,
ran into the woods, and met there.

These were the woods of the Carpathian Forest.
The trees were full with thick leaves.
Vegetation was dense.
Zlata, Junia and the others met their contacts:
Insurgents!
Insurgents were other Jews who were living there.
All were escaped Jews
who were hiding in the forest.
They had formed a small network.

The insurgents brought them to a shallow cave,
a tiny hiding place, called a bunker.
It was on the side of a hill.
Mountains, hills, and dense vegetation
encircled them.

The bunker was hidden amidst a dense mesh of
trees, branches, vegetation, and brush.

Using their bare hands,
they dug deeper into the soil below the bunker.

Now their hiding spot was partly above ground,
and partly below.
They covered the mound of freshly dug soil
with brush.
It must be safe.
If found, they would be shot.

A small trickle of water from a mountain stream
flowed down the side of the mountain.
Their liquid.

Now to remain silent.
Below ground during the day,
quietly above ground during the dark of night
to search for leaves and nuts
to sustain themselves.

They must leave no tracks.
Summer and autumn passed.
Each night, they covered tracks
with leaves, branches, and scrub brush.
Though they felt themselves growing weaker,
they were alive.

The forest saved them.
Though filled with rodents, animals and insects,
it had saved them.

Nevertheless, they lived in constant fear
every minute of every day.
Each as dangerous as the other,
Germans, Ukrainians or Poles might find them.

Winter came with a vengeance.
Bitter cold.
Yet no fire dare be lit for warmth,
lest someone might see it.

Snow drifts were enormous,
and their footprints created deep crevices
that were so difficult to cover.

They could leave the bunker
only during the darkest hours of night.
Only then might they search for food
and for dry straw to cover their emaciated bodies.
After that,
they must devote the few remaining hours
to covering their tracks in the snow drifts,
with branches and scrub brush.

Sometimes, insurgents came to them with potatoes.
Sometimes, they came with news.

Initially, the news was of German liquidation
of Jews within small villages,
or of German penetration into the forest.
Yet, gradually, the news changed.
It was of German military losses to the Russians.

Weeks passed.
One day, insurgents came with frightening news.
The Germans would be combing their region
of the forest the next day!
They were advancing
with a large number of soldiers and military dogs.
Their dogs would be able to find anyone hiding!
They would detect their scent!

Their group,
the three teenage boys, the young woman,
the older couple, and Junia and Zlata must split up.
The danger of being caught was greater
if they remained as a large group.
Blessings shared,
they seperated in different directions,
each running deeper into the forest.

Junia and Zlata ran deeper
into the thick brush of the forest.
Taller trees, larger rocks, higher mountains.

They ran.
They caught their breath.
They ran again.

Finally, they found a small shallow cave.
With bare hands,
they dug a partially subterranean bunker.
They erected a barrier of rocks in front.
Their hands were raw.

They remained in this bunker for weeks.
Then months.
It was all a blur.
A blur of a mother's and her daughter's
fight for survival.

Sometimes,
other insurgents located them.
They told of the gradual defeat of the Germans
and the progress of the Russian army
in battling them.

One day,
although deep in the forest
they heard voices in another language.
The language was not Polish.
Nor was it German.

The Russians had defeated the Germans.
They were reclaiming these lands.

With fear and trepidation,
Zlata and Junia left the safety of their bunker.

Russian soldiers met them.
The war was over.
Germany was defeated.
It was safe for them to return home.

Junia wondered:
Did she have a home?
Her father, sister, and brother-in-law
had been brutally murdered.
Aunts, uncles, and cousins turned in by neighbors,
sent to the Belzec concentration camp,
and then cremated.
What about the others?
Were there any Jews still alive?

The Russian soldiers brought them to Boryslaw.
Jewish homes and businesses had been taken over.
Synagogues burned.
Jews brutally beaten and killed by Ukrainians.
Jews killed, buried alive and cremated by Germans.
Jews turned over to Germans by Polish neighbors.
Was this still her home?

Zlata was forty-four. Junia was sixteen.
Junia took off the white armband from her arm.
The white armband with the blue Star of David.

The town seemed so different.
Local Poles and Ukrainians stared at them,
and then turned their backs.

They went to their home—
the cluster of three houses
that Zlata's father, Isaac Lerner, had built.
The house with the one-room synagogue.

They were yelled at, threatened,
and ordered to get off the property.
It was someone else's home now.
They had no home.

Some Polish neighbors spoke to them,
but feared taking them in.
Anti-Semitism had escalated during the war,
especially amongst the Ukrainians.
Although the Jews were the main victims
of the war,
others blamed them for it.

Junia and Zlata were able to stay, for a brief time,
in the home of Junia's sister's friend, a dentist.
But he could not help them for long.

Returning Jews were despised.
Both returning Jews, and those who helped them,
were in danger.
Over 1,000 Jews who tried to return
to Poland were murdered.
Thousands more were brutally beaten.

Of the 15,000 Jews of Boryslaw before the war,
only 400 survived:
200 survived because Russians sent them to Siberia
before the Germans gained control.
200 survived by hiding.
Poland was not a safe place for Jews.
Junia and Zlata had no home.

They were taken into a Jewish refugee camp.
There, they were sheltered in tents,
fed and clothed.

Nothing, however, could heal the emotional scars.
Nothing could heal the loss.

With the knowledge that the unthinkable,
the worst of all possible nightmares,
had just occurred,
how could they face the future?

By the end of the Nazi Holocaust,
Germans had murdered
seventy percent of European Jewry,
and ninety-eight percent of Polish Jewry.

The physical and emotional needs of the survivors
were enormous.

Zlata and Junia began the legal immigration process
to immigrate to the Holy Lands.

With such an enormous number of refugees
with no money, no identities, and no past,
the process was painfully slow.

NUMBER OF JEWS MURDERED
BETWEEN 1 SEPTEMBER 1939 AND 8 MAY 1945

Due to the extensive nature of the Holocaust, with entire families of Jews being killed, only an estimate of the actual number murdered is possible.

FINLAND
11

NORWAY
728

ESTONIA
1,000

Furthest German Advance

Baltic Sea

LATVIA
80,000

LITHUANIA
135,000

DENMARK
77

MEMEL
8,000

HOLLAND
106,000

DANZIG (Free City)
1,000

SOVIET UNION
1,000,000

BELGIUM
24,387

GERMANY
160,000

POLAND
3,000,000

Ukraine

LUXEMBOURG
700

(Galicia)

CZECHOSLOVAKIA
217,000

RUTHENIA
60,000

AUSTRIA
65,000

HUNGARY
200,000

TRANSYLVANIA
105,000

FRANCE
83,000

RUMANIA
40,000

YUGOSLAVIA
60,000

Black Sea

ITALY
8,000

MACEDONIA
7,122

THRACE
4,221

ALBANIA
200

GREECE
65,000

KOS
120

RHODES
1,700

CRETE
260

LIBYA
562

In the refugee camp,
there were so many needs.

Zlata was appointed director of an orphanage.

During this time,
one of Junia and Zlata's distant relatives,
Ira Katz,
had heard that they were alive.

He began searching throughout the camps
for them.
Finally he found them.

Before the war,
he had been living in a neighboring town in Poland.
During the war,
he was drafted by the Russian army.

Ira fell in love with Junia's gentle soul.
How could he not have?
They wed.

During their three years in the camps,
they began the process of rebuilding their lives.

Zlata Baum

After the Holocaust

In June of 1949,
they left for the United States.

And it was then
that I first met my always gentle
aunt Zlata, and cousins Junia and Ira.

Though I was yet a child,
and though we spoke different languages,
I could not help but feel the love in their eyes,
the gentleness of their smiles,
and the peace of their souls.

I felt it then,
and I have continued to feel it,
every day of my life.

May the story of their survival
and of the innocence of their souls
send a wave of much needed love
around the planet-

A wave that will spread,
and cause a ripple effect
that may touch the hearts of all humankind.

Junia and Ira Katz

In the displaced persons camp
after the Holocaust.

REFERENCES

Brisco, Thomas C. *Holman Bible Atlas*. Nashville: Broadman and Holman Publishers, 1998.

Chameides, Meir. *That War and Me*. Translated by Shula Neufeld. 2001. Unpublished.

Cohn-Sherbok, Dan. *Atlas of Jewish History*. London: Routledge, 1996.

Egit, Jacob. *Grand Illusion*. Ontario, Canada: Lugus Productions. 1991.

Gilbert, Martin. *Atlas of the Holocaust*. London: Michael Joseph Limited, 1982.

———. *Atlas of Jewish History*. 6th Ed. London: Routledge, 2003.

———. Consulting editor. *Atlas of Jewish Civilization*. NY: Macmillan Publishing, 1990.

Horowitz, Irene and Carl. *Of Human Agony*. NY: Shengold Publishers, 1992.

Magocsi, Paul Robert. *Ukraine: A Historical Atlas*. Toronto: University of Toronto Press, 1987.

CPSIA information can be obtained
at www.ICGtesting.com
Printed in the USA
JSHW071955280223
38151JS00016B/3